I am a Quetzalcoatlus

Written by **Karen Wallace**

Illustrated by **Mike Bostock**

Hodder
Children's
Books

A division of Hodder Headline Limited

I am a Quetzalcoatlus.

I am gliding over green forests.

Look through my eyes and see what I see.

A giant Quetzalcoatlus
glides in the sunshine.
His shadow is
wide as a plane
flying over
the ground.

swooping Quetzalcoatlus!

He has wings made of skin.

They fold out like umbrellas.

His bones are hollow like tubes.

Three curling claws hang
from his wrist.

His wings spread from
his ankle to the end
of his fourth finger.
His fourth bendy finger
is twice as long
as his arm.

A sharp-eyed Quetzalcoatlus
spies the gleam of the lake shore.
Others like him are feeding
in the warm silver water.
He flies over the mudflats.
They stretch out like a runway.
The hungry Quetzalcoatlus
glides slowly
and lands.

Giant Quetzalcoatlus!

His neck is long as a ladder.

His legs are high as a lamp post.

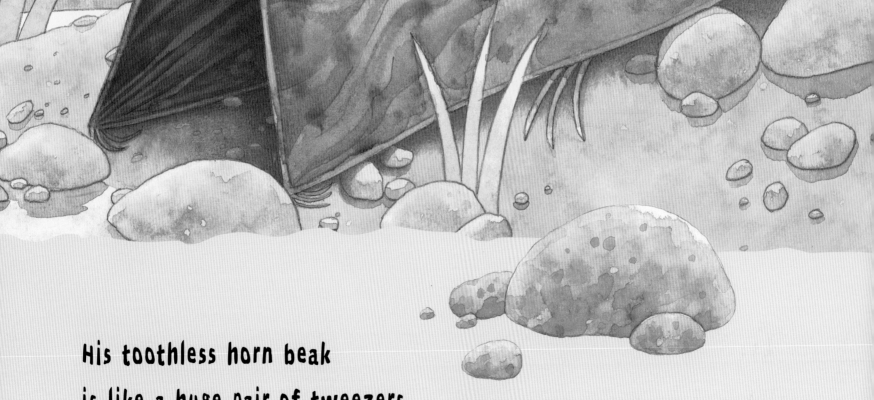

His toothless horn beak
is like a huge pair of tweezers.
He folds back his wings and edges down to the water.

A gust of hot air blows
up from the lake shore.
The Quetzalcoatlus feels
the ground tremble.
He turns his skinny
eyes upward.

The clouds are
orange and purple.
Far, far away,
a volcano explodes.

Long-beaked Quetzalcoatlus
pulls clams from their burrows.
He scoops scrabbling crayfish.
He snaps crabs from the sand.

He knows his mate is
waiting at their nest site.
He will eat as much as he
can before he flies to her side.

The Quetzalcoatlus moves forwards.
Sand swirls around him.

He runs faster and faster
through the hot gritty air.
He spreads his leathery
wings and soars into the sky.

A mother Quetzalcoatlus sits with others on a rock ledge. She is guarding her eggs.

Soon her babies will hatch.

She needs her mate to protect them.

She watches the skies.

Three hungry Dromaeosaurus
leap from a boulder.
Their teeth are curved knives.
Their razor sharp claws are
ready to strike.

The mother Quetzalcoatlus
jerks backwards in fear.
She hears her mate calling
as he flies overhead.

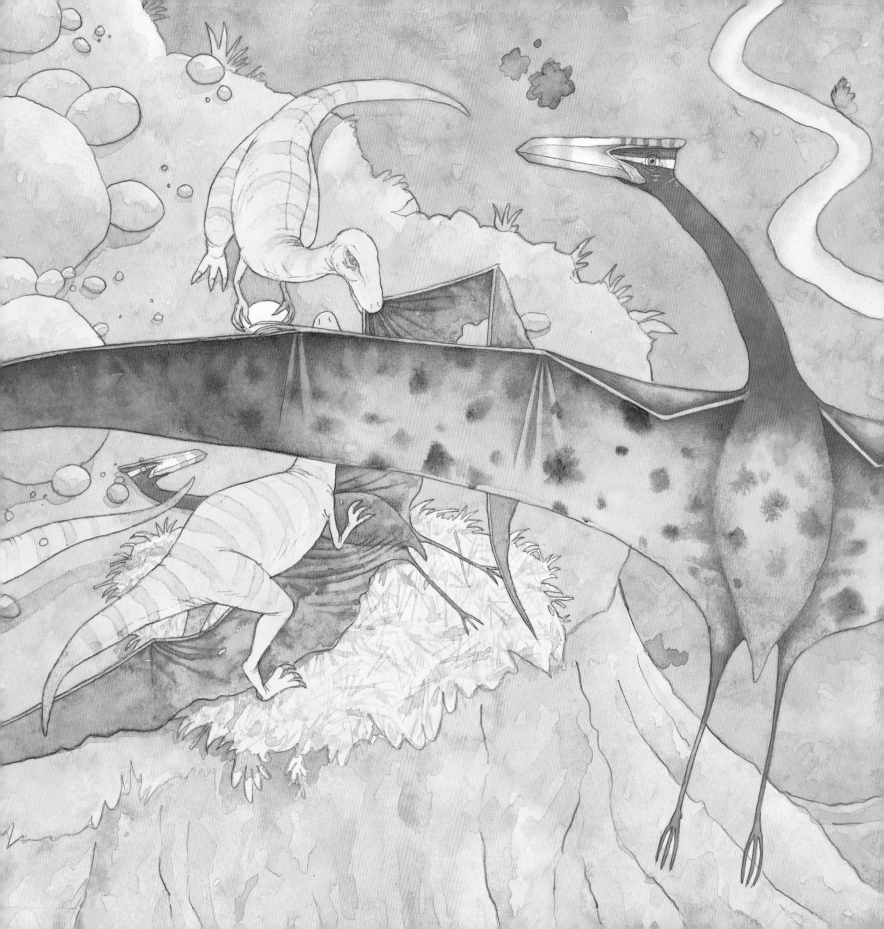

Too late!

The Dromaeosaurus attack.
They swallow eggs whole.
They rip leathery wings.
The Quetzalcoatlus swoops
down as near as he dares.
He sees and understands.
He turns sharply away.

I am a Quetzalcoatlus.

The ground trembles below me.

I glide over the rock ledge and soar into the sky.